POLAROID STORIES

by
NAOMI IIZUKA

An adaptation of Ovid's
Metamorphoses

Dramatic Publishing
Woodstock, Illinois • London, England • Melbourne, Australia

Polaroid Stories was first workshopped site-specifically through The Playwrights Center in Minneapolis, Minn. En Garde Arts also workshopped the play in New York at PS 122.

The first performance was at the Humana Festival of New Plays, Actors Theatre of Louisville, March 1997. Directed by Jon Jory, it included the following cast:

D (dionysus)	SCOT ANTHONY ROBINSON
Philomel	MONICA BUENO
Eurydice	KIM GAINER
Persephone/Semele	DENISE CASANO
Orpheus	BRUCE McKENZIE
Narcissus	MICHAEL RAY ESCAMILLA
Echo	MIRIAM BROWN
G (zeus, hades)	NELSON VASQUEZ
The Lydian Sailor	DANNY SECKEL
Ariadne	CAITLIN MILLER

Scenic Designer	PAUL OWEN
Costume Designer	MARCIA DIXCY JORY
Lighting Designer	GREG SULLIVAN
Sound Designer	MARTIN R. DESJARDINS
Properties Designer	MARK J. BISSONNETTE
Production Stage Manager	DEBRA ACQUAVELLA
Assistant Stage Manager	CIND SENENSIEB
Dramaturg	MICHAEL BIGELOW DIXON
Casting	LAURA RICHIN CASTING

Polaroid Stories was most recently produced by Campo Santo at Intersection for the Arts in San Francisco, Calif., 1998.

POLAROID STORIES

A Play in Two Acts
For 5 Men and 5 Women

CHARACTERS

D (dionysus)
EURYDICE
PERSEPHONE (also SEMELE)
ORPHEUS (also TEREUS)
PHILOMEL
SKINHEADgirl (a.k.a. neon girl)
NARCISSUS
ECHO
SKINHEADboy (a.k.a. oklahoma boy/speedracer)
G (a.k.a. zeus, hades)

Set requirements: Minimal
Approximate running time: 2 hours

ACT ONE
fucked-up love songs

Prologue

(In the darkness, PHILOMEL begins to sing. A fragment of an old song, familiar and haunting. Her voice is solitary, unadorned, childlike. The sound of the streets grow around her voice: traffic like the ocean, trains rumbling underground, a pay phone ringing and ringing, pieces of radio, a bass line, glass shattering, a faint siren faraway. In a sea of noise, PHILOMEL's song is gradually lost.)

THE FATE OF THE LYDIAN SAILOR
the story of oklahoma boy

(A small light in the darkness. Shadows like fish underwater. A light. D appears, a figure in the darkness.)

D. this is how it begins, this is where—
     i seen him out of nowhere, crazy amped-out boy
       crazy oklahoma boy,
     i found him up by port authority,
     scheming and scamming, nickel diming what he can—
     i watch him awhile, see him get all's he can get,
     and then he goes, he gets high on spray. oklahoma
       boy likes spray.
     spray's cheap, he says, and then he smiles like a psy-
       chopath.

tell you what, he says to me, i ain't got a friend in
   this whole world,
are you my friend, he says to me,
what you got for me, friend? i got a kingdom, i says
   to him,
behold my kingdom,
and he thinks that's the funniest thing.
he laughs so hard he falls down.
and then we get high. we fly.

oklahoma boy likes speed,
he likes it cause it makes him go so fast it makes him
   go fucking speedracer fast with them fucking speedracer eyes.
one night, he rips me off, digs around till he finds my
   stash,
i hear his fingers, i hear his eyes clicking in his head,
   i hear him laughing in the dark
so high he can't hardly stand, he can't hardly breathe,
and then he takes my stuff, he goes away—
pockets full of quarters, he finds some arcade, video
   world is all there is all there ever was,
oklahoma boy disappears for days,
all speedracer eyes, big eyes, black as night, full of
   laser beams and showers of light, galaxies and plan-
   ets, whole worlds exploding in his head, and it's so
   bright,
what it is, right, it's so bright, for a second you think
   you can see then all there is is black—

(Darkness.)

A LIST OF MINOR GODS AND GODDESSES

(Voices in the dark call out from every direction. Sometimes the voices cut each other off. Sometimes they overlap. A sea of names spoken fast and loud. The names are statements, taunts, teases, fighting words.)

M3. my name is bandit
F1. my name is tina
M2. my name is blondboy
M1. My name is ramon
F2. my name is mohawk girl
F3. my name is lupe
M4. my name is viper
F4. my name is lisa j
M5. my name is crazy todd
M1. my name is ninja b
F5. my name is desiree
M2. my name is david c
F1. my name is rochelle
M3. my name is tiny
M4. my name is paco
M5. my name is skater pete
F2. my name is mai thai
F3. my name is baby punk
M1. my name is tiger
M2. my name is little ray
F4. my name is candy
F5. my name is loca
F1. my name is skinheadgirl
M3. my name is baby j
M4. my name is nazi mike

M5. my name is tweeker shawn
F2. my name is nothing girl
M1. my name is oklahoma boy
F3. my name is jamie b
M2. my name is zero
M3. my name is shadow
M4. my name is scratch
M5. my name is nicky z
M1. my name is dogboy
M2. my name is skinhead steve
F4. my name is happy girl
M3. my name is marco
M4. my name is psycho john
F5. my name is melody
M5. my name is scarface
M1. my name is kaos
F1. my name is disappear

(The voices reverberate, echo. And then there is silence.)

HOW EURYDICE CROSSES THE RIVER OF FORGETFULNESS
the journey between two worlds

(EURYDICE is crossing the River of Forgetfulness. She walks through the water. Ancient trash floats across the water's surface, which gleams black as oil. PERSE-PHONE waits for her on the other side. She is the queen of the dead.)

EURYDICE. my name is disappear. my name is disappear.

PERSEPHONE. hey! who do you think you're talking to,
    disappear?
EURYDICE. i'm talking to anybody who's listening
PERSEPHONE. is that right?

EURYDICE.
    i'm talking to somebody who knows how it goes—
    you know how it goes, i know you do, too—see it in
    your eyes. so you tell me then, cause i want to
    know, tell me about the places i've never been to,
    tell me about all the places i'm gonna go to

PERSEPHONE. don't you start that song with me, little
    girl

EURYDICE.
    i said to him, this town is too damn small for me
    this town ain't good for nothing—
    i want to get out of here
    i want to see the world
    i want to see some fireworks in this life, is what i said
        to him

PERSEPHONE. you ain't telling me nothing new, nothing i
    ain't heard before

EURYDICE.
    i want to be famous
    i want to sleep in satin sheets

PERSEPHONE. girl, please

EURYDICE.
>i want to dance and dance all night long
>i want to go someplace in this damn life, is what i
>said to him—

PERSEPHONE. heard that, heard that, heard that all before

EURYDICE.
>but see, it's like this: i got a man like a bad dream
>follows me no matter where i go

PERSEPHONE. heard that, too

EURYDICE.
>i feel his eyes on my back
>i feel his breath on my neck, no matter how far i get
>to

(ORPHEUS appears out of the shadows, approaches.)

EURYDICE.
>and he's all
>shut up, you ain't going nowhere, what are you think-
>ing, girl, who are you kidding?
>and i'm looking at him
>and all i can think is
>who
>are
>you
>to
>me?
>who were you ever to me?

    like you matter to me
    like anything you say is going to make a difference to
       me
    like i want to stay in that nowhere town doin nothing
       all my life
    like i want to be with you forever
    like i want that

PERSEPHONE. little girl
EURYDICE. i ain't no little girl
PERSEPHONE. little girl is all you are—
EURYDICE. i ain't no little girl, all acting like you know
me
PERSEPHONE. i know you, little girl. i know you like i
know myself.

*(ORPHEUS comes so close to EURYDICE, a chain
fence is all that separates them.)*

ORPHEUS.
    what are you thinking, little girl—
    —you ain't going nowhere—

EURYDICE. —you can't touch me—
ORPHEUS. —is that right—
EURYDICE. —where i'm going to, baby, you ain't never
going to find me—
ORPHEUS. —shut up—
EURYDICE. —how do i look walking away?
ORPHEUS. —you ain't walking away—
EURYDICE. —how do i look walking away from you,
baby, how do i look to you—

(ORPHEUS tries to follow her. He climbs the fence and falls, crashing to the ground.)

ORPHEUS. baby—

EURYDICE. i take the bus across a thousand miles

ORPHEUS. i can see you

EURYDICE. i sleep i sleep

ORPHEUS. i can see the veins under your skin, i can see your heart beating

EURYDICE. i sleep i sleep, i sleep like a dead person. it's like i disappear. and when i wake up, i'm a thousand miles away, and it's all like "where you from, you got a place to stay, how'd you like to come spend the night, how'd you like a little of this, how'd you like a taste just a taste, come on, baby, this shit is good—"

PERSEPHONE. ain't nothing new, i know how this goes:

ORPHEUS. hey, girl

PERSEPHONE. "hey, girl"

ORPHEUS. i'm talking to you

PERSEPHONE. "hey girl"

ORPHEUS. i'm talking to you

PERSEPHONE. "yeah, i'm talking to you—you got a name? where are you from? you got a place to stay? you need a place to crash awhile—hey—"

ORPHEUS. hey, girl—i'm talking to you, ain't nobody else in the world but you—

PERSEPHONE. "how'd you like to spend the night, how'd you like a little of this"

ORPHEUS. i can see you. baby, i can see straight through you.

PERSEPHONE. "how'd you like a taste, just a taste"

ORPHEUS. don't you walk away from me

PERSEPHONE. "come on, baby, this shit is good"

ORPHEUS.

> don't you walk away from me when i'm talking to
> you—
> hey—hey, i'm talking to you—bitch—

*(The sound of a woman singing through a sea of static
snow. ORPHEUS tries to climb the fence one more time.
He falls, crashing to the ground, tries to climb again
and again.)*

EURYDICE.

> you look like someone who knows how it goes, so
> i'm going to tell you how it goes,
> i'm high, right, and this guy
> he says to me, where are you from—bitch—
> he wants to touch me, get inside of me, know every-
> thing about me.
> he wants to know how i got all these scars on my
> pretty little body.
> i tell him, sweet as i know how: baby, i forget.
> i drink from the river of forgetfulness.
> i forget the names i forget the faces i forget the stories
> i forget all kinds of shit.
>
> when he's asleep, i roll him, i kick his ass, take his
> cash, take his fancy watch
> and i'm looking at him
> and all i can think is
> who are you to me,
> like you know me

like you think i'm going to tell you the truth
like you think i'm going to give you that—

yeah, baby, i got scars
i got scars all over, but i don't even know this story,
  see.
ain't no story, cause i forget.

(EURYDICE gets to the other side of the river and dis-
appears with PERSEPHONE into the darkness. On the
other side of a chainlink fence, on the other side of the
river, ORPHEUS watches EURYDICE disappear. He has
blood on his hands from where the chainlink cut his skin.)

THE STORY OF NARCISSUS
gazing in the mirror

(NARCISSUS is a skinny, beautiful boy in dirtied-up
rave wear. ECHO is a runaway girl, plain and un-
washed.)

NARCISSUS. yeah, so, how it goes, right, how it goes is
  like: and then and then
ECHO. and then and then and then and then
NARCISSUS. it's like it's like
ECHO. it's like it's like
NARCISSUS. it's like this, check it out: i meet this guy,
  right, and we go to his place and it's phat it's plush
ECHO. it's phat it's plush
NARCISSUS. it's all glass and chrome
ECHO. glass and chrome

NARCISSUS. black leather, plush pile, big-screen tv with surround sound

ECHO. surround sound

NARCISSUS. mirrors everywhere, on the walls, in the hall, on the ceiling, looking at myself

ECHO. looking at myself

NARCISSUS. and we're kicking back, and it's cool

ECHO. it's cool

NARCISSUS. and he's like, are you hungry? and i'm like, yeah, i'm hungry, and so we order in, and i eat steak and eggs and fries and some pizza and all this ice cream and shit, and i'm eating like a pig cause i'm starvin

ECHO. i'm starvin

NARCISSUS. and we're drinking all this wine, and he's like, this is nice wine, and i'm like, yeah, it's ok, nothing special

ECHO. nothing special

NARCISSUS. and he busts out this big fat doobie, and i'm like, all right, and we get high

ECHO. we get high

NARCISSUS. and i say to him, dude, if this is the high life, dig, the high life is ok by me, and that makes him laugh so hard, and i see his teeth like tiny pearls all shiny white, and i'm like, dude, you are so ugly

ECHO. you are so ugly

NARCISSUS. and he laughs, and he's like, how about a movie, so he pops in a tape, and it's like scarface, and it's like my favorite movie, i love that movie, that movie is so excellent

ECHO. so excellent

NARCISSUS. "say hello to my little friend"

ECHO. "little friend"

NARCISSUS. and i'm like kicking back, watching the movie, and i'm so high, i feel like i'm coming out of my skin, and i look up at this mirror and i see the dude, he's on his knees, and he's like sucking me off, and i can't even move, and al, my man, he's like blowing all these punks away, a whole fucking army of em, booyah booyah, and i'm so high, this chump's giving me head, and i'm just like, whatever

ECHO. whatever

NARCISSUS. and then later, dude gives me some cash, and he's like, hey, this was fun, and i'm just like, uh huh yeah whatever

ECHO. whatever

NARCISSUS. see ya—chump

ECHO. chump

NARCISSUS. and then i'm out of there, i'm gone—

(NARCISSUS goes. ECHO follows. Darkness.)

PHILOMEL'S STORY
fucked-up love song

(PHILOMEL is singing in the darkness, an ancient song filled with nostalgia and longing. ORPHEUS listens. He cannot see the singer, though he hears her song. A siren from faraway approaches. PHILOMEL stops. Then silence. The siren passes, fades into the night.)

ARIADNE IN THE LABYRINTH

(SKINHEADgirl moves through the darkness. An echo chamber, voices and laughter bouncing off cement, the origin impossible to gauge. Stuff spills out of SKIN-HEADgirl's bag, a string of things.)

SKINHEADgirl. hey. hey. are you there? can you hear me? *(Silence.)* hey. hey, it's me—quit fooling, say something— *(A long, high whistle in the dark. The sound of beer cans clattering on cement. Shower of beer.)* hey— hey— *(Silence.)* man, i swear when i find you i'm going to kick your ass. for real i am *(Laughter and voices resonate. An echo chamber.)* yeah, you think this some kind of goof, you think this some kind of big fat joke, well, fuck you, cause i ain't laughing, i'm sick of your stupid-ass games, fuck you, man, fuck you—

(A storm of noise. SKINHEADgirl moves on into the darkness. A match is struck. A small light in the darkness. D and the SKINHEADboy. SKINHEADboy is whistling, making noise in the dark. His voice echoes through the space. The echoes delight him.)

D. behold my kingdom
SKINHEADboy. tss. kingdom of shit
D. behold my castle, my mansion, my taj mahal
SKINHEADboy. man, this place is a pit. it fucking stinks in here.
D. man, you stink
SKINHEADboy. hey, fuck you

D.   i stink, too. yeah, i do, and that's the truth.
      but, see, i like the stink. it smells of home.

SKINHEADboy. home? man, this ain't no home.
D. this is my home.
SKINHEADboy. that is so fucked up. anybody tell you
   how fucked up you are?
D. i ain't fucked up, i'm a god
SKINHEADboy. tss, you're a goddamn wingnut
D. i'm a god, and that's a fact. this is my kingdom. wel-
   come to my kingdom, oklahoma boy
SKINHEADboy. that ain't my name
D. skinhead boy
SKINHEADboy. dude, i ain't no skinhead
D. it don't matter to me what you are.

SKINHEADboy.
      i ain't no skinhead. that ain't my trip.
      see, check it out.

*(SKINHEADboy shows him crude lettering tattooed in-
side his arm.)*

D. "fuck na zi scum."
SKINHEADboy. see, now, that's the real deal. for real for
   real. this girl i know, she did this tat for me. i got my ass
   kicked in eugene, oregon, on account of this tat. six
   skinhead brothers, fucking twelve steel toes. i almost
   kicked it that time, truly i did.
D. "fucking twelve steel toes." bullshit.
SKINHEADboy. hey, fuck you. you believe what you
   want. just don't be calling me no skinhead. freak.

D. little brother, i'm a god

SKINHEADboy. yeah, whatever

D. so what do you want this god to call you by, little brother

SKINHEADboy. you call me whatever you want. it don't make no difference to me. it ain't like i'm going to be around that long.

D. is that so?

SKINHEADboy. that's a fact. i'm outta here monday. i got a plan. i got it all set up. i hate this city, man, this city is bunk. till then, you know, i'm just killing time.

D. so, what if i call you speedracer

SKINHEADboy. tss

D. speedracer—now that's a rad-ass name, fucking demon on wheels

SKINHEADboy. yeah, no shit. fucking demon on wheels.

D. you like that?

SKINHEADboy. speedracer is where it's at, and you know it, too. speedracer flies, man, he goes so fast, he goes so fucking fast, zero-gravity fast, feel his head explode— pow powpow pow pow

D. hey yo, speedracer

SKINHEADboy. yeah, that would be me

D. you want to get high, speedracer?

SKINHEADboy. hell yeah, i want to get high.

D. speedracer likes to fly

SKINHEADboy. damn straight

D. he likes to go real fast

SKINHEADboy. he likes to go so fast, till he's like a blur, and nobody sees him, nobody can get near him, nobody can touch him, and then he's gone

D. i hear that, i know what this is

SKINHEADboy. for real for real. so bust it on out. what you waitin for? let's have us a party. i feel like a party.

(In the darkness, D and SKINHEADboy get high. In that same darkness, PHILOMEL slips through and follows the trail of things that spilled out of SKINHEADgirl's bag. She picks up a small transistor radio and turns it on. The sound is scratchy and old. She switches stations. A collage of radio fragments. They grow louder. PHILOMEL listens, captivated.)

ORPHEUS AND EURYDICE
the wedding feast

(PHILOMEL's love song turns into music from a boombox. The sound of laughter. EURYDICE and ORPHEUS. At the foot of a chainlink fence. Remains of a fast-food feast.)

ORPHEUS. ok, ssh, ssh. check it out, i love you
EURYDICE. ok, ok, hold up. ok. i love you
ORPHEUS. i love you
EURYDICE. i love you
ORPHEUS. i love you
EURYDICE. i love you.
ORPHEUS. i love you.
EURYDICE. goof
ORPHEUS. how much do you love me?
EURYDICE. i don't know, goof
ORPHEUS. how much?
EURYDICE. i don't know. a lot.
ORPHEUS. like about how much?

EURYDICE *(spreads her arms as far as they will go).* like about—this much

ORPHEUS. yeah?

EURYDICE. times a hundred million billion

ORPHEUS. that's a lot

EURYDICE. that's a hella lot

ORPHEUS. i love you on account of your true loveliness

EURYDICE. oh yeah?

ORPHEUS. on account of your hella pure heart

EURYDICE. tss—i love you on account of your goofiness

ORPHEUS. yeah?

EURYDICE. on account of your goofy freakiness

ORPHEUS. uh huh

EURYDICE. on account of your snooty groovy wackiness

ORPHEUS. i love you

EURYDICE. yeah, i love you, too

ORPHEUS. for real?

EURYDICE. yeah

ORPHEUS. i mean it, for real?

EURYDICE. yeah, sure

ORPHEUS. say it then

EURYDICE. for real—goof

ORPHEUS. when you sleep, i read your mind. it's like we're lying real close, skull to skull, and our brains meld, they become all siamese twin like, and i'm like sucking the thoughts right out of your head, swirling them around, seeing how they taste

EURYDICE. yeah, and how do they taste?

ORPHEUS. good

EURYDICE. yeah?

ORPHEUS. juicy

EURYDICE. yeah?

ORPHEUS. juicy fruit

EURYDICE. juicy fruit

ORPHEUS. passion fruit. brain juice

EURYDICE. that is so nasty

ORPHEUS. it's the flavor, it's the key flavor

EURYDICE. oh, is it key?

ORPHEUS. it's so key

EURYDICE. tss—baby, you are too much fun

ORPHEUS. yeah? you havin fun?

EURYDICE. yeah, i'm havin fun

ORPHEUS. are you happy? do i make you happy?

EURYDICE. i don't know. i guess

ORPHEUS. i make you feel good?

EURYDICE. sure

ORPHEUS. i make you feel like nothing else?

EURYDICE. yeah sure whatever

ORPHEUS. so like what are you thinking right this second?

EURYDICE. i don't know—nothing

ORPHEUS. come on

EURYDICE. read my mind

ORPHEUS. no, i'm askin you

EURYDICE. no, i'm serious—read my mind—

ORPHEUS. —i'm askin you—

EURYDICE. —suck my thoughts right out of my head—

ORPHEUS. —i'm askin you—

EURYDICE. —come on, brain juice man—

ORPHEUS. —i'm askin you—

EURYDICE. —brain juice juicy fruit passion fruit—

ORPHEUS. —shut the fuck up—fuck

EURYDICE. ok, ok. see, what i'm thinking, what i'm thinking is: you are so like this guy i used to know back home—man, i couldn't get far enough away, i couldn't

put enough miles between—this was a thousand years
ago—look like him, talk like him, fucked up in the head
just like him—i look at you, it's like i'm looking at him.
ORPHEUS. i love you. i love you—
EURYDICE. —yeah whatever
ORPHEUS. i love you, for real
EURYDICE. hey look, i gotta go—
ORPHEUS. —wait—
EURYDICE. i got shit to do, baby, i got all this shit to take
care of—
ORPHEUS. —hold up—
EURYDICE. —i'll see you around, ok, i'll see you real
soon, i promise— *(Goes.)*
ORPHEUS. hey. hey, wait—fuck—

(ORPHEUS follows her. Darkness.)

PROMETHEUS STEALS FIRE
a song of whispers

*(Darkness. The sound of things crashing. The sound of
breathing. Light on SKINHEADgirl and SKINHEADboy.
He's rifling through D's things, looking for D's secret
stash, trashing everything. SKINHEADgirl watches.)*

SKINHEADgirl. —fucking big man, fucking full of plans,
fucking thinks he knows everything about everything
SKINHEADboy. fuck
SKINHEADgirl. "don't worry, baby, you wait here, i'll be
back, i got it covered, i'll take care of you, trust me,
baby"—my ass

SKINHEADboy. shut up

SKINHEADgirl. you shut up—and that's the last time you leave me like that, get high on my time, cause i ain't goin to come looking for you next time, and i sure as hell ain't going to wait around till you sleep it off—asshole—

SKINHEADboy. —i saw him put it right here, i saw him

SKINHEADgirl. well, it ain't there now

SKINHEADboy. fuckfuckfuck

SKINHEADgirl. give it up—it ain't there—

SKINHEADboy. —shut up—

SKINHEADgirl. —quit telling me to shut up—

SKINHEADboy. —i know it's here, i saw him stash it, i saw him— *(Sounds in the labyrinth.)*

SKINHEADgirl. —shit—ok, come on, let's go—let's go, what's wrong with you—

SKINHEADboy. —shut up—

SKINHEADgirl. —we got to go, come on, i want to get out of here, i want to go, i'm scared—

SKINHEADboy. —just shut up—

SKINHEADgirl. —fuck you, i'm scared *(SKINHEADboy retrieves a bag from the gash in the wall. It rips. Colored pills fall, scatter. They are like jewels—emeralds, rubies, sapphires, opals—pharmaceutical treasure. He grabs as many as he can.)*

SKINHEADboy. holy shit—i told you, i fuckin told you—

SKINHEADgirl. —ok all right, let's go, please, let's get out of here—come on—

(SKINHEADboy and SKINHEADgirl run. Darkness.)

PHILOMEL'S STORY
transistor radio song

(In the darkness, SKINHEADgirl is running for her life. The headlights of passing cars cut through the darkness and then disappear into the night. They catch her in the glare and then lose her again, like a strobe. Her footsteps and her breathing are gradually swallowed by the sounds of traffic, trains rumbling underground, voices, laughing, a pay phone ringing and ringing, glass shattering. The sound of breathing, like a pulse. ORPHEUS emerges from the darkness. He's looking for EURYDICE, but she's nowhere to be found. He finds PHILOMEL's radio on the ground, picks it up, puts it to his ear. The love song from before is playing faintly. It grows louder. ORPHEUS listens for a moment. PHILOMEL watches him. ORPHEUS looks up and sees her watching him. Music from a passing car, thundering bass. It drowns out all the other noises. Darkness.)

THE STORY OF SEMELE
a bedtime story

(Faint salsa music. PERSEPHONE is transforming into SEMELE, the woman she used to be. In the darkness, SEMELE tells stories to her unborn child. D sees her when he dreams. He sees her now, though she never sees him. In his dreams, he can never make her see him.)

SEMELE.
    story of a girl who turned into an echo

story of a girl who turned into a shooting star
story of a girl who crossed the river of forgetting
how she crossed the river of forgetting, and never
   came back
story of a girl who fell in love with a god—

(The salsa music begins to distort, becoming something foreign and strange. D approaches SEMELE.)

D. And how this god, how he loved her back

SEMELE. loved her so much he promised to give her anything she asked for, anything in the world

D. and she said to him, i want to see you. i want to see you for real. i want to see you as you truly are. that is my wish

SEMELE. and the god, he said, wish for something else, anything else. but she didn't want nothin else, and so he kept his promise, and when she saw him, she saw how he was pure fire. so bright, like the sun in the sky, and when she touched his face, she burned

(D is so near to SEMELE he can almost touch her. And then bright light like a flash. The music ends. Darkness.)

THE STORY OF SEMELE
a magic trick

(SEMELE stares into the dark. Inside of her is a baby, an invisible pulse. G is watching her.)

SEMELE. what? what are you looking at? don't just stand there like you're made of stone, cause you ain't made of stone. damn, say something.

G. girl, you are so sweet, you are so fine—

SEMELE. —tss—

G. —"you are so fine, you blow my mind." see, girl, you are the one, you are my queen, my lady love—

SEMELE. —save all that. see, cause i know what it's worth.

G. what can i say to make my girl smile? what kind of love song can i sing to her? what kind of magic words can i say to her to make her open up for me like some kind of beautiful flower—

SEMELE. look, i ain't gonna play this game with you. where's my stuff?

G. baby, all i got for you is love, ain't nothing deep, ain't nothing special. love is what it is. simple as a shoe.

SEMELE. baby, i don't need no goddamn shoes.

G. all right, girl, how about i give you my heart?

SEMELE. your heart? is that what you just said to me?

G. yeah, it's a big meaty heart. what more can you want from a man?

SEMELE. try, say, a big-screen tv, try, say, a jeep cherokee and a trip to miami beach with the sunshine and the palm trees and the white sand and the ocean so blue you can see every goddamn fish there is, and no fleabag motel, i want luxury accommodations, first class all the way

G. is that all you want from me?

SEMELE. oh no, baby. that ain't it, uh huh. what i want, dig, what i want is love, love, love, tss—

G. what the fuck's the matter with you?

SEMELE. let go of me—

G. girl, how much shit do i got to swim in to get to you?

SEMELE. you're hurting me. *(G lets go.)* yeah, you best let go of me, fuckin kick your ass, fuckin kill you. love— fuck that. i don't want none of your love. tell you what i want. truly. enough rock to do me for eternity. i want a snow mountain, my own beautiful snow mountain, and i'm the only one knows where it is. i climb this mountain and i disappear. i get lost in more white than i can ever dream of. *(G turns to go.)* baby? baby, wait. baby, don't go. baby, i'm sorry, i'm sorry. i love you, right, i love you. yeah, i do. you know i do. you the one. you the only one. i love to be with you, be close to you, i love you, you know i do— *(G and SEMELE embrace.)* baby?

G. yeah?

SEMELE. baby, you love me back?

G. yeah.

SEMELE. yeah, you do?

G. yeah, i do.

SEMELE. baby, where's my stuff? i know you got it, you can tell me—

G. —later—

SEMELE. —tell me now—

G. —i'll tell you later—

SEMELE. no, you tell me now.

G. what?

SEMELE. where's my stuff? fuck. where's my fucking stuff? tell me now, you tell me now, fuckin tell me now— *(SEMELE goes after G with her hands. She tries to tear him apart.)* fuck you. you love me, huh?

G. yeah.

SEMELE. how much do you love me?

G. you know how much. why are you askin me?

SEMELE. because i want to hear you say it. say it.

G. with all my heart.

SEMELE. what would you do for me?

G. anything. you know that.

SEMELE. then you give me my stuff. if you love me, give it to me.

G. don't ask me that. ask me for anything else.

SEMELE. ain't nothing else, ain't nothing else 'cept how much you love me. how much do you love me?

(G gives SEMELE her rock, and she smokes it up. The smoke rises and envelops SEMELE. Like some girl in a fucked-up magic trick.)

THE BIRTH OF D
smoke

(SEMELE is dancing in the smoke, faint and faraway. In the darkness, the sound of strangers breathing, coughing. the faint sound of salsa. G is in the shadows. As he speaks, SEMELE continues to dance. She is turning back into PERSEPHONE. By the end of her dance, she is once again PERSEPHONE. As PERSEPHONE, she disappears into the darkness.)

G. i used to love this girl. this was a thousand years ago. i seen her in the park, and she's dancing with some other guy, and he's playing some kind of salsa kind of music, and it's summer, and she's wearing some little dress with flowers, and she's dipping and turning, smiling at nothing, just smiling, the sweetest smile— i tell her, "baby, you are the one, you are my lady love, you are my queen. ask me anything, girl, i'm like a god. i have powers—anything you want in this world, i can get it for you. just ask me to, and i will." but she don't want nothing else.

(The salsa music grows louder. It becomes distorted. D appears. He has been watching and listening.)

G. i used to love this girl, and she and me, we had a son. i seen him one time before i go away. little boy, beautiful boy, tiny fists and eyes shut tight, shakin, his whole body shakin, shakin so hard, like he's filled with all kinds of strange dreams.

(G recedes into darkness.)

BACCHIC SONG

(The sound of a woman singing through a sea of static snow. AM radio in the late-night hours. An ancient recording, scratched and crackling. PHILOMEL begins to sing, a live voice alongside the radio song. EURYDICE emerges and dances by herself. She dances as SEMELE danced, an echo of another woman. ORPHEUS appears and approaches EURYDICE. The two dance together.)

D.   Stories she told me, whispered to me like secret things, before i was born, before i even remember—
      story of a girl who turned into an echo

story of a girl who turned into a star
story of a girl who fell in love with a god
and how she died and crossed the river of forgetting,
how she heard this girl on the crossing, stranger on
  the other side,
how this girl, how she sang this song—
sad song
love song
some kind of fucked-up love song—

(ORPHEUS' and EURYDICE's dance turns into a struggle. EURYDICE breaks away and goes.)

PHILOMEL'S STORY
wordless song

(The sound of breathing underneath PHILOMEL's singing. A pulse. The pulse grows. ORPHEUS is alone. He sees PHILOMEL. She stops singing. The sound of breathing. A pulse.)

ORPHEUS. girl, what are you looking at? why are you looking at me like that? what do you see when you look at me? tell me. what did you see? what did you see in me?

(ORPHEUS moves toward PHILOMEL. PHILOMEL flees. ORPHEUS follows her. As he hits the chainlink fence, a sudden explosion of techno music—a bass line, a woman singing, looping back on itself like a record stuck in a groove. Bursts of light like shooting stars.

Bodies moving in the darkness. They are like shadows
underwater, caught for a second in slivers of light, body
parts, then swallowed by the dark.)

MOVING THROUGH THE LABYRINTH
stuck in a groove

(Techno music underneath. In the labyrinth. Inside the
labyrinth, a monster is breathing. Voices from different
corners of a dark space call out. SKINHEADboy and
SKINHEADgirl are moving through the labyrinth. Shad-
ows.ECHO is an echo, an aural illusion.)

SKINHEADboy. hey
ECHO. hey
SKINHEADboy. hey
ECHO. hey
SKINHEADgirl. hey
ECHO. hey
SKINHEADgirl. hey
ECHO. hey
SKINHEADboy. hey
ECHO. hey
SKINHEADgirl. hey
ECHO. hey

(SKINHEADboy disappears in the labyrinth.)

SKINHEADgirl. hey
ECHO. hey
SKINHEADgirl. hey

ECHO. hey
SKINHEADgirl. hey
ECHO. hey

(SKINHEADgirl disappears into the labyrinth. ECHO follows her. The music changes. A pulse. ORPHEUS appears. He stares into the darkness. He sees shadows, figures he thinks he recognizes.)

ORPHEUS. hey *(An echo.)* hey *(An echo.)* hey.

(ORPHEUS disappears into the labyrinth.)

ARIADNE IN THE LABYRINTH

(Techno music underneath. The sound of breathing. An echo chamber. The sound of a boy and girl running, shrieks and laughter echoing. Silence. The sound of hard breathing. SKINHEADgirl is tripping out in the darkness.)

SKINHEADgirl. hey. hey. where did you go, where the fuck did you go? *(A sound, a whistle.)* i can't see *(A sound, a whistle.)* i can't see, i can't see—fuck you, i can't see

(SKINHEADboy comes up behind SKINHEADgirl, grabs her.)

SKINHEADboy. yo, wake up, bitch

SKINHEADgirl.
>fuck you. i hate you.
>don't you fucking laugh at me.
>man, you are such an asshole.

SKINHEADboy. what's the matter? you scared?

SKINHEADgirl. no, i ain't scared

SKINHEADboy. bullshit

SKINHEADgirl. go to hell

SKINHEADboy. you were out-of-your-mind scared just now

SKINHEADgirl. i wasn't.

SKINHEADboy. you lie you lie. *(SKINHEADgirl girls starts tripping again.)* hey. hey. what's wrong with you?

SKINHEADgirl. nothing.

SKINHEADboy. you lie.

SKINHEADgirl. whatever—

SKINHEADboy. what?

SKINHEADgirl. i don't know. i don't feel good.

SKINHEADboy. tss. you are such a lightweight.

SKINHEADgirl. fuck you

SKINHEADboy. you're such a girl

SKINHEADgirl. man, fuck you

SKINHEADboy. nah, it's cool, it's cool cause i'm around, and i'll be there, right, i'll be there to love and comfort you—

SKINHEADgirl. shut up

SKINHEADboy. girl, for real, you are so lucky i'm around.

SKINHEADgirl. is that right?

SKINHEADboy. hell yeah. cause i'm the man of your dreams, girl. i'm the shit.

SKINHEADgirl. oh yeah, are you the shit?

SKINHEADboy. you know it. i'm the one's going to save you from the monsters.

SKINHEADgirl. tss. ain't no monsters, not for real.

SKINHEADboy. girl, you don't know what you're talking about. you're ignorant.

SKINHEADgirl. you're so fucked in the head.

SKINHEADboy. hah, shut up, cause you don't know. this is the darkness

SKINHEADgirl. hey—

SKINHEADboy. this is where the monsters live.

SKINHEADgirl. ain't no monsters. not for real.

SKINHEADboy. girl, they're real. and they're all over, too, hiding out, waiting. we can't see them, but they see us, girl, they're looking at us, laughing at us, they want to fuck with us, rip us off, but i ain't going to let that happen, see, cause i got a plan, i know how it goes, i'm watching out, i watch my back, i keep moving, ain't nothing going to catch me, i'm fast, i'm so fuckin fast— girl, i go so fast, i fly, i'm like a blur, i'm like invisible.

(SKINHEADboy's voice gets fainter and fainter as he speaks. The darkness closes in, warm and immense, and wraps SKINHEADgirl in its folds.)

SKINHEADgirl. ain't no monsters. not for real. i don't believe in fairy tales. i don't believe in magic shit. i don't believe in monsters. ain't no monsters, not for real. ain't no monsters 'cept the ones in your head. hey. hey. where are you? where did you go? say something. *(Silence. SKINHEADgirl is alone in the darkness.)* man, fuck you. i'm sick of your stupid-ass games. *(A sound in the dark-*

ness.) is that you? hey. hey, are you there? say something—

*(SKINHEADgirl turns around. A sharp intake of breath
like a girl about to dive underwater. Darkness.)*

THE STORY OF NARCISSUS
an echo

*(Techno music underneath. NARCISSUS is stranded.
He's drinking a forty [oz. beer] by himself. ECHO keeps
him company, at a distance. He ignores her.)*

NARCISSUS. what? what are you looking at? cause, girl, i
ain't no tv show. what? what? what are you looking at?
tss.

ECHO. tss.

NARCISSUS. fuck it.

ECHO. fuck it.

NARCISSUS. forget you

ECHO. forget you

NARCISSUS. girl, don't you be fuckin with me. cause i
ain't in no mood, right. what? what? fuck. ok, you want
to know how it is? yeah? you want to know how it goes?
ok

ECHO. ok

NARCISSUS. ok. so this is how it is, this is how it goes
for real. i see this guy tonight, right, this guy i used to
know, city, and i see him, and he's coming out of this
lincoln towncar and he's this old guy, right, but he's
looking good

ECHO. looking good

NARCISSUS. built, nice suit, the hair

ECHO. the hair

NARCISSUS. and i see him from across the street, right, and so i cross like four lanes of traffic and i'm running to catch up, and these cars are all honking at me, and finally i get right up next to him

ECHO. i get right up next to him

NARCISSUS. an i'm walking next to him, and he's walking fast, and i'm like close enough i can smell his skin

ECHO. i can smell his skin

NARCISSUS. i can smell the gel

ECHO. i can smell the gel

NARCISSUS. in his hair

ECHO. in his hair

NARCISSUS. and i'm like, hey, man—

ECHO. —hey, man—

NARCISSUS. —what's up—

ECHO. —what's up—

NARCISSUS. —where you been—

ECHO. —where you been—

NARCISSUS. —what's going on, what's happening—

ECHO. —what's happening

NARCISSUS. and i'm talking to him just like that, nothing deep, and everything's cool

ECHO. everything's cool

NARCISSUS. but it's like this guy, right

ECHO. this guy

NARCISSUS. he don't hear me, so good, so i keep talking and talking

ECHO. —talking and talking

NARCISSUS. and i'm talking so loud, it gets so like i'm
    shouting, i'm practically shouting in this guy's ear, and
    finally i'm just like, damn, you must be going deaf, old
    man, you must need a fucking hearing aid or something,
    and right as i'm saying this, right, this big fat guard, he
    comes out of this building, he's all telling me, take a
    walk, man, do yourself a favor, get lost, and i'm like
    "shut up, rent-a-cop, ain't nobody talkin to you," and
    i'm lookin at this guy i used to know, right, and he's just
    standing there, and he don't say a word. it's like he's
    looking right through me, it's like i ain't even there, and
    finally i'm just like, fuck it, this ain't worth my time,
    this asshole, he ain't worth my time, none of this is
    worth my time—tss. who am i talking to? i don't even
    know why i talk to you—girl, get out of my face, get
    lost. i said, get lost, disappear—

*(NARCISSUS tosses his empty. Glass breaks. ECHO
goes. Darkness.)*

ORPHEUS' LOVE SONG

*(Techno music underneath. Late night. ORPHEUS has
been drinking for a long time. He's looking through a
chainlink fence at EURYDICE. As he speaks, she approaches.)*

ORPHEUS.
    i love you like a hurricane
    i love you like a moth loves fire
    i love you like a sweet perfume

    i love you like a fucked-up flower
    i love you like a dog loves bones
    i love you like a bear loves honey
    i love you like a bird loves sky
    i love you like a big hot sun
    i love you like a ball and chain
    i love you like a dumb love song
    i love you like a cold hard drink
    i love you like a secret key
    i love you like a superhero
    i love you like a sad-faced clown—you look so pretty

EURYDICE. you're drunk

ORPHEUS. these are the ways i love you

EURYDICE. freak

ORPHEUS. i'm writing you a love song. i'm writing it in
    blood like an oath

EURYDICE. don't bleed for me, don't even

ORPHEUS. cross my heart. hope to die, stick a needle in
    my eye— i'm going to win back your heart, swear i will

EURYDICE. baby, i'm heartless, ain't you caught on yet

ORPHEUS.
    i love you like a burning fever
    i love you like a crown of thorns
    i love you like a hungry lion—

EURYDICE. —give it up, chump

ORPHEUS. it's like i have loved you forever into eternity
    and back, it's like i knew you from another life

EURYDICE. oh yeah?

ORPHEUS. it's like we were joined together in this other life, we had different names—see, we were different people, we had completely different lives, different destinies —you know what i'm saying—but you knew me and i knew you, and we fell in love, and we got married and shit

EURYDICE. and then i died

ORPHEUS. no, see, you ain't dead

EURYDICE. dead to you, freak

ORPHEUS. you went away, you know, for a little while. you needed your space and shit, but you'll come back. girl, i know you will.

EURYDICE. i died, baby. i went to hell. that's my new address—you gonna come visit me in hell, baby?

ORPHEUS. i'm going to come bring you back.

EURYDICE. tss. i got news for you, i don't want to come back.

ORPHEUS. i know that ain't true.

EURYDICE. this is my life, right here, and you don't know what i want, you don't know me

ORPHEUS. i'm going to rescue you

EURYDICE. tss, in your dreams

ORPHEUS. i'm going to follow you to the ends of the earth, to the afterlife

EURYDICE. i really ain't got the time for this—

ORPHEUS. —hold up, hold up, wait a sec—

EURYDICE. —i gotta go, i'm outta here— *(Starts walking away. ORPHEUS follows her alongside the fence.)*

ORPHEUS. —you're always fuckin outta here—

EURYDICE. —i ain't got time for this, i ain't got time for you—

ORPHEUS. —and what is that supposed to mean? what're you doing that's so fuckin important?

EURYDICE. —man, curl up and die—

ORPHEUS. —what is that, what is that? why are you always so fuckin smart with me?

EURYDICE. —i said, drop dead—die, freak— *(Walks away.)*

ORPHEUS. baby, i know you don't mean that, i know you don't. girl, can you hear me? girl, i'm talking to you. i'm going to rescue you, see, i'm going to pull your ass outta the flame, i'm going to rescue your ass—hey. hey. where are you going to, where the fuck are you going to, don't you walk away from me—bitch—

(ORPHEUS tries to follow her. He climbs the chainlink fence and falls, crashing to the ground. EURYDICE disappears in the darkness.)

THE STORY OF SEMELE
medusa song

(Techno music underneath. The sound of a girl breathing. Late night. PERSEPHONE is trashing a public bathroom. Outside, voices and laughter. The slam of a stall door. Then silence. A mirror. PERSEPHONE speaks to a reflection, wasted.)

PERSEPHONE. yeah yeah yeah, fuckin song sung blue—tss. so what do you want to know about me, cause i'll tell you everything, right, i got a thousand stories to tell, and i'll tell them for free, i'll fuckin give them away. so what it is, right, i had a baby. he ain't with me now or anything. i gave him up. i was pretty messed up at the time, but that's a whole nother story. when he was born, my baby, he had something wrong with his heart, with the way his heart was put together—fuck, i don't know. it's been so long, you know, i forget. anyway, it ain't like i think about him every day or anything—it ain't even like that. just sometimes, i think about where he is now, you know, and what he looks like, if he looks like me, if he remembers me, stupid shit like that.

(ECHO comes upon PERSEPHONE. She notices ECHO, looking at her in the mirror.)

PERSEPHONE. yeah, what are you looking at? i see you looking at me, like you got some kind of problem. you got a problem? what the hell are you looking at? you want to piss me off, bitch? you better get out of my face before i kick your ass, cause i ain't none of your business to be looking at—what are you looking at, huh, what the fuck are you looking at—

(ECHO goes. PERSEPHONE gazes at her reflection and slowly turns to stone.)

PHILOMEL'S STORY
blood song

(Techno music underneath. PHILOMEL emerges from an empty building onto the street. The sounds of the street—traffic, a telephone ringing, glass breaking, a siren. The sound of breathing. A pulse. PHILOMEL opens her mouth. No sound comes out. Blood instead of sound.

*She touches the blood with her fingers. And then touches
the chainlink fence, the cement, the walls. And everywhere her fingers touch, she stains the world red. In the
darkness, the red turns into blood-red flowers. Techno
music grows louder.)*

THE STORY OF PENTHEUS (Book III)

*(Techno music underneath. SKINHEADgirl is sleeping.
She's been sleeping for a long time. SKINHEADboy is
dancing in circles to boombox music. He's wearing a
long platinum wig. D watches him. The music stops. He
stops dancing.)*

D. hell, don't stop, man. you just got into some kind of
groove.

SKINHEADboy. fuck you—

D. oh man, you got the flair, you got all the moves, you got
it all down

SKINHEADboy. shut up—

D. i watch you, too. i like it. i like to watch you dance.

SKINHEADboy. i said, shut up, faggot. fuck this shit anyway, stupid shit. *(Takes the wig off and chucks it. D
picks up the wig and puts it on.)*

D. how do i look?

SKINHEADboy. fucked up.

D. yeah? you think so?

SKINHEADboy. yeah, i think so. tell me, why are you so
fucked up? how'd you get to be that way?

D. little brother, i ain't fucked up enough. i ain't even close.

SKINHEADboy. born to fry, born to die, born to lose

D. tss

SKINHEADboy. yeah, what's your problem, faggot?

D. man, you make me laugh.

SKINHEADboy. oh yeah—faggot? tell you what, some faggots i'd like to kill.

D. yeah, is that right?

SKINHEADboy. i see them sometimes on the street or something, and i see them looking at me, all checking me out, and i know what they're thinking, too, and i'm thinking to myself i'd like to kill one. fucking cut one up, come up from behind, and slice him.

D. yeahyeahyeah

SKINHEADboy. kicked the shit out of some old geezer last night. he shit his pants. he smelled so bad. he didn't even have a dime. you think that's funny. you think i'm funny.

D. yeah, i think you're funny, man.

SKINHEADboy. yeah, well, fuck you, too

D. what's the problem, funny man?

SKINHEADboy. ain't got no problems. ain't you noticed. i'm fuckin carefree.

D. tss. you feel like getting high, funny man?

SKINHEADboy. yeah, whatever

D. i know you feel like gettin high. man, you always feel like gettin high.

SKINHEADboy. i said, whatever.

D *(looking for his stash hidden in the walls).* what's up with girlfriend?

SKINHEADboy. i don't know.

D.   she sick?
      she dead?

SKINHEADboy. who the fuck knows, man. i don't know what's wrong with her, like i'm supposed to know her story.

D. maybe girlfriend got a little greedy. maybe girlfriend huffed a little too much joy.

SKINHEADboy. what she is ain't none of your business, man, she ain't none of your business, so just shut the fuck up about her. *(To SKINHEADgirl.)* yo, wake up, bitch. i said, wake up. wake up wake up, fucking wake up.

D. hey hey hey—relax

SKINHEADboy. man, i am so relaxed. you don't even know. i'm so goddamn relaxed right now, i'm fuckin bored. don't nobody ever tell you how boring all this shit can be. hey same ole same ole. gets so i feel like taking somebody down, just to hear the way they sound, the way their body sounds, just to hear their heartbeat, just to know they ain't all fuckin zombies staring right through you like you ain't even there. damn, i fuckin hate this place.

it stinks of piss.

it's cold.

it's dirty.

i'm fuckin sick of this place.

but, see, what it is, i got a plan, right

i got it all worked out

i ain't about to let shit get me down, i ain't about to let nothing get me down, cause i know what i'm do-ing, and i got it all figured out

D. somebody been in my stash, somebody ripped me off.

SKINHEADboy. yeah? man, that's too bad.

D. yeah—tss. yeah, it is.

SKINHEADboy. we're going, you know. like in the morning. for real, man. she's got family in pennsylvania. her mother's sisters. cousins and all her cousins' kids. it's a big fucking family, they live out in this place called rome. i never heard of it. out in the goddamn country. fields and farms and shit. she got us bus fare, me and her. and when we get out there, we're going to get us jobs, get us some money together, and then we're going to get married and like that. that's what it's going to be like for us. man, i didn't take your shit.

D. be real with me now

SKINHEADboy. i didn't take nothing from you

D. because the thing being this: i see in the dark, i read your mind

SKINHEADboy. it's this fucking city, man

D. can't turn your back

SKINHEADboy. this city is bunk

D. can't trust nobody

SKINHEADboy. i fucking hate this city, man. this city is all fucked up. it's full of thieves and fuckin perverts

D. junkies and drunks. speed freaks. everybody's wet for something. sweet sweat. man, you smell like you been speeding.

SKINHEADboy. get out of my face, faggot

D. how fucked up are you now?

SKINHEADboy. i ain't fucked up. i told you that.

D. how dumb do you think i am?

SKINHEADboy. listen, man, you're my friend. i don't steal from friends, right. that ain't my trip.

D. boy, you are so full of shit.

SKINHEADboy. yeah, and what do you know about me, talking shit about me like you know me, like you got that right

D. you don't care about nothing 'cept getting high, i know that much

SKINHEADboy. i didn't take a fucking thing from you.

D. don't lie to me. ain't nothing i hate worse than a liar.

SKINHEADboy. i ain't a liar, faggot. you watch how you talk to me. i could kick your ass.

D. what did you say to me?

SKINHEADboy. i could kill you.

D. ain't about dancing around. ain't about talking big. you got to touch me to kill me. we got to be that close.

SKINHEADboy. yeah? you feel like dying, you feel like dying tonight, faggot?

(Darkness. And then pieces of light. D is holding SKIN-HEADboy up against the wall. The light cuts up his body. Chest, arm, neck, mouth. Pieces of skin. D whispers to him like a lover.)

D. listen up, baby, this faggot is a god. my daddy was a god and so the fuck am i. my momma, she wanted to see a god up close, she wanted to feel that thing. she burned, boy, so you be careful what you say to me, you show me some respect. now, did you take my shit? answer me.

SKINHEADboy. no.

D. boy, what do you take me for? who do you think i am?

SKINHEADboy. man, fuck you. you ain't nothing to me. ok, so i ripped you off, and i'd rip you off again. i ain't scared of you.

D. who do you think i am, punk, stealing from me? i could
    kill you with my hands.
SKINHEADboy. bring it on, man, cause i don't care. fuck
    you. cause i ain't scared, i ain't scared.

*(Darkness. In the shadows, D breaks SKINHEADboy
into a thousand pieces. The sound of blows. The sound
of breathing. Light. SKINHEADboy is alone in an ocean
of darkness. The face of a boy. The sound of breathing.
A pulse.)*

SKINHEADboy.
    i ai't scared, i ain't scared
    i ain't scared, i ain't scared
    i ain't scared, i ain't scared—

*(The sound of a woman singing faintly. The sound of
breathing.)*

SKINHEADboy. i was born in grand island, nebraska, west
    of omaha. my mother was this beautiful queen like in
    some kind of fairy tale. i don't know what my father
    was. i forget his name. he skipped town when i was like
    a baby, went to denver or something. when i was seven,
    some guy my mom was shacking up with tied a rope
    around my middle and put me in this well out back. he
    wasn't angry. he wasn't nothing. it wasn't like that. i
    stayed in the well for eight days. i couldn't see in the
    dark. i didn't never think about dying. i listened. i
    waited. i heard the sound the trees make, the way they—
    ssh. and the bugs in the ground, rubbing against the dirt,
    whispering. and the water, the way the walls bled water

was this sound, so much sound. later, my mother was holding me. she was breathing so close to me, warm and wet, her face so close to me. she kept saying, i'm sorry, i'm sorry, i'm sorry like it was the words to some song. she held me so tight it hurt. she held me like i was coming apart.

(Darkness. The bottom of a well. Buried in a mother's embrace. The sound of breathing.)

PHILOMEL'S STORY
lament

(Outside on the street, bodies disperse, going in separate directions into the night. The smell of weed and sweat, the sound of glass breaking, the sound of voices growing fainter. PHILOMEL sings in the darkness. She has no tongue. She sings in a foreign language filled with nostalgia and longing. A siren from faraway approaches. PHILOMEL stops. Then silence. The siren passes, fades into the night.)

END OF ACT ONE

ACT TWO
polaroid stories

THE MYTH OF PROTEUS

(Light. NARCISSUS talks into the light. An interview with a stranger.)

NARCISSUS.

all right all right, here it is, all right, check it out:

how i got on the streets is like this:

it's like this: once upon a time, like a long time ago, i was left in this dumpster outside phoenix, i was like a little baby, nobody wanted me, and then this pack of wild dogs dug me out, fed me, took care of me, taught me how to hunt and shit, i didn't know what human was—ok ok never mind, that's b.s.

how it is, it's like this: i fell out of the sky over salt lake city, utah—

no wait, it's like this: i washed up on the shore of the mighty mississippi—

no wait, it's like this: i was left for dead in a room in palm springs

i was left for dead in a room in las vegas

i was left for dead in a parking lot in tucson

i was left for dead on the steps of the fucking lincoln
memorial—

no wait up, wait up, that ain't how it goes—

ok, check it out, it's like this: i was left for dead in
this stripmall outside san ysidro, right, and this poor
mexican family found me, and took me back over
the border to tj, and raised me as one of their own
nah. that ain't true neither, i'm just playin you.
what really happened, it's like this, and this is for real—

when i was like a little kid, the building where i lived
at, it caught on fire, mmhm, and my mother, she
held me out the window, and she was all like: "fly
away fly away fly away, little bird," and then she let
go—only thing was, i wasn't no little bird, and i
didn't fly, i fell, and i don't know what the bitch
was smokin, cause if i didn't die from the fire, i
shoulda straight up died from the fall—'cept the
thing being i landed on this big old mattress somebody threw out with the trash—fuckin fate, man,
was on my ass—and then later this old wino found
me, and took care of me for a while till his liver gave
out, and then i was on my own, i was all alone, and
that is the truth, i swear to god—

(Darkness.)

G AND EURYDICE
zeus seduces a maiden

(Night. EURYDICE makes her way through the darkness. G watches her.)

G.   hey, baby, hey, sugar,
       where you goin to, sweet thing, pretty thing?
       hey, baby, i'm talkin to you. don't you know how to
       talk? what's a matter with you, sweetheart? ain't you
       got no tongue?

EURYDICE. come again, old man?

G. i said: ain't you got no tongue.

EURYDICE. old man, everybody's got a tongue. some
    folks, they know how to keep it from flapping around all
    the time. some folks know how to give it a rest.

G. girl, i know what you're saying.

EURYDICE. oh yeah, you know what i'm saying? tss.

G. yeah, i do, see, i knew a girl with no tongue, for real.
    some crazy guy she knew, he cut it right out of her head
    with a knife.

EURYDICE. —man, that's some sick shit that i don't need
    to be hearing—

G. —baby, this story ain't even what you think it is. this
    story's got one happy-ever-after, righteous ending. see,
    some god up high, he saw that girl, saw how her tongue,
    how it got cut out, and how she bled, and in his heart, he
    felt for her, and turned that girl into a bird, songbird, and
    she sang this crazy fucked-up song, so strange and true,
    folks couldn't help but stop and listen.

EURYDICE. man, i don't believe any of that.

G. girl, believe it. see, i been all around, and i seen all kinds of crazy shit go down.

EURYDICE. tss, whatever you say, old man.

G. i ain't that old, baby, you better take another look. *(EU-RYDICE looks. G smiles and it's like sun through the clouds.)* what's your name, sweetheart?

EURYDICE. i forget.

G. come on, baby, what's your story? where you come from, where you headed, where you been?

EURYDICE. baby, i forget.

G. baby, you forget a lot.

EURYDICE. baby, i have drunk from the river of forgetfulness. i forget the names, i forget the faces, i forget all kinds of shit—

G. girl, you forget what you want to forget.

EURYDICE. hell yeah, i do.

G. but see now, some things, they don't let you forget. they mark you, no matter how far you run, no matter how far you get. *(Gently touches the side of EURYDICE's face. His voice is a whisper, a spell that stops her in her tracks.)* it's like i look at you, and what i see, right, i see all these scars. girl, i see so many scars, new ones over old, some ain't even mended yet, and i'm thinking to myself, how does a girl get all them scars, how does that happen to somebody she ain't even grown yet. i want to know their story, baby.

EURYDICE *(moves away)*. you're out of luck, old man. ain't no story, cause i forget.

G. now i know that's a lie, i know that for a fact.

EURYDICE. old man, get away from me. i ain't playing with you no more.

G. baby, i got scars myself, more than i can even count. i can still feel each one, i can feel the way the skin's gone all see-through, like if you looked real hard, you could see straight inside me.

EURYDICE. you lived to tell, huh?

G. always, baby. i'm like a god, can't snuff me out.

EURYDICE. you lookin for a date, or what?

G. i'm lookin for something.

EURYDICE. what you lookin for, baby? you lookin for a little love?

G. i'm lookin for something.

EURYDICE. something is a lot of things.

G. what you got to give?

EURYDICE. old man, i ain't got nothing to give, ain't nothing free in this life.

G. now that's the hard truth. i like a woman who tells the truth. you always tell a man the truth?

EURYDICE. it ain't like i'm makin no promises.

G. no promises, no lies. ain't that how the song goes?

EURYDICE. i'll tell you what, old man, if you know all the words to that song, you ain't as dumb as you look.

G. tss. how about you take a little walk with this old man, kill a little time—come on, sweet thing, pretty thing, what you got to lose?

(EURYDICE follows G into the darkness.)

INCIDENTAL TRANSFORMATIONS
songs orpheus sings to the queen of the dead and D

(Darkness. The sound of voices and laughter. D, PERSE-PHONE, and ORPHEUS. The remains of fast-food wrappers and beer bottles. ORPHEUS is humming.)

PERSEPHONE. man, shut up!

ORPHEUS. how about i tell you a little story about love—

PERSEPHONE. tss. i ain't listening to none of that. cause, see, baby, i'm done with love. love, for me, that's fuckin ancient history. for real, what's some story about love goin do for me?

ORPHEUS. make you smile

PERSEPHONE. tss

ORPHEUS. make you cry

PERSEPHONE. baby, i got plenty to cry about. i don't need no story to make me cry.

D. what up? you got a story, jack? you got somethin you dying to say?

ORPHEUS. yeah, i got something i want to say. see, what it is, it goes like this: this guy i used to know, he loved this girl, but she didn't give him the time of day. she thought she was hot shit, she thought she was all that.

D. tss. heard that, jack. heard that all before. that story is so old.

ORPHEUS. man, i wasn't talkin to you. that story was for the lady.

PERSEPHONE. baby, that girl was a fool, and a fool stays a fool no matter what. why should i give a damn about what happens to some fool?

ORPHEUS. baby, all of us are fools

PERSEPHONE. but that was one fucked-up story though, huh?

ORPHEUS. but see, baby, that's how love goes most of the time

PERSEPHONE. tss, seriously. tell me somethin i don't already know by heart

D. ok, all right, listen up, i got one for you—girl, are you listenin?

PERSEPHONE. oh yeah uh huh, yeah i'm listenin—i'm hangin on your every word, baby, i can't wait—

D. i'm serious, don't be giving me none of that. you listen up, cause you goin like this one: story of a man who loved to love too much. he loved the girls so much, but he was old, dig, and the girls, they'd be all like, "old man, get away, you're too old for me—" but he didn't care, he told them: "girls, i ain't a man, i'm a god, and a god can turn into any damn thing he pleases. he can turn into the gold chain dangling around your neck, he can turn into the red cherry candy melting in your mouth, he can turn into some racy, lacy thing you wear right up close against your skin—"

PERSEPHONE. —man, shut up, cause that is so nasty—

D. —that old man had something going on, see, he was cagey and sly, ticklin and touchin, squeezin and kissin, getting all the love he could get, and that old man, he found love in some of the strangest places, sniffed it out like some old hound dog, and i swear, he lived happily ever after, the end.

PERSEPHONE. tss, sounds like the story of one dirty old man.

D. baby, you miss the point entirely. that man was sly, he had a plan—

ORPHEUS. give it up, man. that story sucked.

D. yeah, what do you know, jack?

PERSEPHONE. what i wanna know is why is it any way the girl's always gotta be a fool?

D. tss. i don't know for sure, but, baby, i can guess—

PERSEPHONE. —don't you go there, baby, cause you won't like it one bit—

D. —see, cause girls, dig, girls are fools when it comes to love—

PERSEPHONE. —you ain't no girl, baby, what's your excuse?

D. —tss—anyway—

PERSEPHONE. —fool—

D. —anyway—how about it girl? you got a story or you just giving me sass

PERSEPHONE. yeah, i got a story. i got one better than all y'alls. story of a man who couldn't keep it in his pants, and how his woman got so sick of it, she got a little potion from this haitian girl she knew, found her old man's little missy, put that potion in the little missy's drink, turned that little missy into a pit bull bitch—beautiful little bitch, all sleek and chocolate brown, staring out at the world with these sad, dog-girl eyes. everybody was all like, "where'd you get that dog, that's a nice dog," but she didn't say a word. tied her up in back with a big old chain, and that bitch, i'm telling you, she howled night and day. heard tell later, she ran away, nobody knows where she got to in the end.

D. is that a true story?

PERSEPHONE. what'd i say? hell yeah, it's a true story

D. tss. i don't believe a word

PERSEPHONE. baby, you best believe what i say, cause i know it all

ORPHEUS. you know it all, huh?

PERSEPHONE. everything and then some

D. tss

PERSEPHONE. ain't nothing i ain't heard of, i've heard it all before

ORPHEUS. baby, i got a story i bet you ain't heard. true story.

D. man, ain't no such thing as a true story. and this girl, here, she lies

PERSEPHONE. —man, shut up.

ORPHEUS. this story is true, story of a man who loved this girl so much he followed her straight to hell. brought her back alive, too, tricked the devil, sang a song, made the devil cry

PERSEPHONE. tss. what kinda song would that be, that would make the devil cry?

D. must have been some kinda very special song

PERSEPHONE. uh huh

D. must have been some kinda crazy-ass song

PERSEPHONE. uh huh

D. must have had the devil shakin and groovin

ORPHEUS. no, man, that ain't how it was, it wasn't like that: the man, he sang this song, all about how he loved his girl, more than money, more than pride, more than his own sorry-ass life—one love, powerful love—and the devil, when he heard the song, he cried, from someplace deep in the pit of his heart, he cried, and all the lost souls in hell, they cried, too, so that all hell echoed with their crying, saddest sound the man ever heard, cause they knew that song, they knew it in their bones,

and what it was to have this pure, precious thing, to have
and to hold in your hands, and then to lose it, you wasn't
even thinking right, and you wasn't holding on, cause
you're stupid and fucked up, and you could've done
things different, but you blew it anyway.

D. damn. man, what are you trying say? cause, see, no of-
fense, but that story sucked. and if that story is true,
man, tss, my name is mud—

PERSEPHONE. —well, then fuck you, your name is mud,
mud.

D. my name ain't mud, bitch.

PERSEPHONE. —why don't you get lost, mud—

D. —shut up, bitch—

PERSEPHONE. —and don't be callin me bitch—

D. —anyway—

PERSEPHONE. —fuck you, bitch, party's over—

D. —anyway then, i guess i'm going now—

PERSEPHONE. —yeah, you're going now, you got that
right, unless you want to be gettin into it, you better get
out of here—

D. tss. right. i'll see you later then. i'll see you around,
jack. later for you, too—bitch *(Goes.)*

ORPHEUS. fuck him

PERSEPHONE. you got that right

ORPHEUS. forget him

PERSEPHONE. forget who?

ORPHEUS. there you go. how about i tell you another little
story about love

PERSEPHONE. yeah, baby, i'm listenin, tell me all about
love, tell me all about that shit, i'm all ears.

HOW SKINHEADGIRL TURNS INTO A STAR
the story of ariadne

(In darkness. SKINHEADgirl wakes up from a deep sleep. She is alone. Her bag has been gone through. Her things are spilled all over. She looks for her stuff, but it's all gone. SKINHEADboy is gone.)

SKINHEADgirl. fuck—fuckfuckfuck—i can't believe this, i can't believe this shit— *(She throws her stuff against the wall.)* i don't care, i ain't scared, cause i'm like this princess in this fairy tale, this fuckin rad-ass fairy tale and i don't get scared ever, cause the princess always lands on her feet, she always ends up ok in the end, for real, yeah, she does. *(She is holding it together. She begins winding through the labyrinth. Her words are a thread to guide her through the dark.)* once upon a time, once upon a time, once upon a time, this princess, she falls in love with this guy named roger, cause roger, he was like her first love, man, roger was her knight in shining armor, he was her prince, and they woulda lived happily ever after, too, 'cept that roger, roger turned out to be this total headbanger freakazoid freak, listenin to deep purple in his momma's basement all day long, full of bullshit about the end of the world. loved to smoke weed. roger was a pig for weed—man, she ended up hating that guy. on the road, the princess met up with chilly, and the princess, she kinda liked chilly—she got chilly willy tattooed on her in honor of him. on her ankle. little tiny chilly willy. cost her forty bucks, too. chilly was sweet, but he had real bad teeth. his teeth, they were all blue. she said to him, chilly, man, why are your teeth blue? what kind of freak are you to be having blue teeth? later, she found out chilly was drinking bleach for the buzz—not enough to kill him, just enough to turn his teeth blue. later they all fell out, every single one. guy was nineteen and not a tooth in his head. the princess left chilly on account of the teeth thing, cause the teeth thing, that was just way too deep.

after that, the princess met jesus. she met him hitching back from wisconsin. she gave him shit on account of that name. she said to him, no white guy is named jesus, not for real, but she liked him, she really did. he was tall and he had long arms he could wrap around her, and he smelled like peppermint, and the princess, she thought he was like the real deal, until the night he ripped her off, and left without a word, and then she realized jesus probably wasn't even his real name, and he was just another loser like everybody else she ever knew, and she was so deep in the shit this time, there wasn't nobody going to be able to bail her out, cause she was shit out of luck, she was truly fucked—no, hold up, that ain't how it goes, that ain't it—fuck. fuck.

(SKINHEADgirl slowly becomes only a voice in the darkness.)

SKINHEADgirl. once upon a time, speedracer, he comes along from straight out of nowhere, and he rescues her, and they live like happily ever after, and all that—fuck. never mind. that ain't it, that ain't how it goes. and after a while, the princess, she just stops, i just stop, and it's like i've been here all my life, and i begin to feel some piece of something, something big as the whole night sky, heavy and full, like how the air gets right before a storm, all electric-like, closing in on me, darkness all around me, and inside the dark, inside the inside, i see all these lights, tiny and sparkling, thousands and thousands of lights, like stars in some far-off galaxy, and i'm thinking to myself, how beautiful they are, and i'm so close i can almost touch them, so close, i can't even tell where i stop and where they begin—

(SKINHEADgirl slowly turns into a star, bright and glowing, a neon girl, a constellation in a sky full of stars. She lights up the dark, flickers, and then burns out. Darkness.)

THESEUS IN THE LABYRINTH

(Darkness. The sound of water dripping. Eyes watching. SKINHEADboy is moving through the darkness. He's bruised. His clothes are dirty and torn. D is watching.)

SKINHEADboy. hey. hey, girl, it's me. you sleepin, you still sleepin? —yo, wake up, wake up—girl, i know you're here, i know you are. come on, girl, say something. just say something, hey—

(A sound. SKINHEADboy thinks he sees something moving fast, a light, on the periphery of his vision. But when he turns, there's nothing there. He runs away. Darkness.)

THE STORY OF ECHO AND NARCISSUS

(NARCISSUS is looking in his mirror—a little girl's mirror encased in bright red plastic, salvaged from somebody's trash. He slowly puts on eyeliner, lipstick. He looks tired and drawn like he's been awake for a thousand long nights. ECHO watches NARCISSUS.)

NARCISSUS. yeah? what? what are you looking at?
ECHO. nothing
NARCISSUS. what? what are you looking at, what?
ECHO. nothing
NARCISSUS. "nothing"—i'm going to start calling you nothing girl. nothing girl with nothing to say, nowhere to be, nothing worth nothing to nobody. you got a smoke for me, nothing girl—i know you do—give it up, give it here— *(ECHO gives him a cigarette. NARCISSUS lights up, sucks in smoke.)* tss, menthol. menthol sucks. i knew this guy back in l.a., smoked egyptian cigarettes. that guy was so fucking loaded. girl, he had so much blow. dude has this red ducati, beautiful machine. we rode down to baja. we'd go so fast. i felt like my head was about to come off. the wind'd make me cry, and he'd look at me and laugh, he'd say—are you sad, little man—but i wasn't sad for real, it was just the wind. what? say it.
ECHO. nothing

NARCISSUS.
     i got a sugardaddy
     i got plans
     i got the keys to a room uptown

i got a thousand dollars in my pocket right now
(you don't believe me, fuck you)
and i can sing, i got a beautiful fucking voice—
i'm going to have a party in my new place real soon,
   and i'm going to get high high high, me and all my
   girlfriends—what?

ECHO. nothing
NARCISSUS. don't be looking at me like that. always
   checking me out—
ECHO. i ain't doing that—
NARCISSUS. —you think i'm hot—girl, you want me, i
   know you do—
ECHO. —you don't know what i want—
NARCISSUS. —who are you kidding, girl? please. follow-
   ing me around, staring at me all the time—you want to
   jump my bones, but that ain't going to happen, not in
   this lifetime, that's for sure—
ECHO. i don't want nothing you got.
NARCISSUS. oh yeah, is that right, is that a fact—
ECHO. —that's a fact. all skinny and bony and shit—
NARCISSUS. —fuck you—ain't like you're anything any-
   body's gonna want to be looking at anyway, so just
   don't even—
ECHO. —shut up—
NARCISSUS. —and, girl, get away from me because you
   smell—
ECHO. —shut up—
NARCISSUS. —i can smell you way over here—
ECHO. —shut up—

NARCISSUS.
>—it's like this, dig, you got an ok face, you got an ok
>body—
>—you ain't beautiful, but it ain't like you're ugly.
>i'm saying you ain't butt ugly
>i'm saying you ain't an all out hound
>i'm saying you ain't a total skank
>i'm saying you ain't half bad—what? what?

ECHO. nothing.

NARCISSUS. oh fuck. relax. it's a joke is all, what's your
problem? what?

ECHO. nothing.

NARCISSUS. girl, you got a thin skin. that ain't no way to
be. that ain't the right attitude. look at me. think posi-
tive. believe in your own self, believe you are all that,
like they say—be all that you can be. how do i look?
what? what? fucking say it.

ECHO. you look nice.

NARCISSUS. fuck you. i look more than nice. i look beautiful. i look at myself, and i think, girlfriend, i am looking at the man of my dreams.

>i got a sugardaddy
>i got plans
>i got the keys to a room uptown
>i am so beautiful and i got a body that will not stop
>and i can sing, i got a beautiful voice—

ECHO. yeah, you do. you got a beautiful voice

NARCISSUS. yeah, i do. i know i do.

ECHO. you could be like a star. i know you could.

NARCISSUS. girl, i'm on my way—star search, dig? i'm all over that shit—man, ed mcmahon, he ain't even heard nothing like me before. i sing like a fuckin angel. what?

ECHO. nothing.

NARCISSUS. girl, you say that to me one more time, i swear i'm gonna scream. and why are you always lookin at me like that?

ECHO. like what?

NARCISSUS. like what, like what—like that. sad. you got sad eyes.

ECHO. what do i have to be sad about?

NARCISSUS. oh, girlfriend, don't even get me started. all kinds of shit.

ECHO. but see i ain't like you.

NARCISSUS. yeah? and what is that supposed to mean?

ECHO. i don't know.

NARCISSUS. "i don't know."

ECHO. i don't.

NARCISSUS. "i don't."

ECHO. fuck you.

NARCISSUS. ok, fuck me, fine, fuck me, whatever. only don't be all like "nothing—i don't know." i swear to god, one day all that's gonna be left of you is just this little voice saying "nothing—i don't know."

ECHO. shut up—

NARCISSUS. —whatever—

ECHO. it's like, it's like, it's like you see all these things, it's like you look out into the world, and you see all this shit, and you're like: i want that and that and that, it's like it ain't never enough for you. as long as you got eyes in your head, it's like you're always wantin shit.

NARCISSUS. girl, i deserve the moon, i deserve the stars, i deserve all of it.

ECHO. yeah, well, i ain't like you.

NARCISSUS. what's wrong with wantin shit? no, i'm serious. what's so wrong with wantin shit? tss. forget this. forget you. *(Starts to go. ECHO follows. NARCISSUS turns again to go.)*

ECHO. it's cause there ain't no point—

NARCISSUS. what? there ain't no point in what? say it, just fuckin say it.

ECHO. there ain't no point in wantin shit you ain't never gonna get.

NARCISSUS. Come again. what am i never gonna get? you think i'm just some kind of fuckin blowhard? is that what you think? is that what you think when you look at me? girl, you must think i'm some kind of sorry-ass loser—

ECHO. —that ain't what i mean, i didn't say it right—

NARCISSUS. —no, you said it right, and i heard it right, too—

ECHO. i don't know what i'm tryin to say.

NARCISSUS. —just shut up, all right?

ECHO. cause you do have a beautiful voice, i've heard you, and i know you could be a star, you could totally be a star, and i'd be so happy for you, too. i'd be like somebody who knew you when, i'd be like somebody you used to know. and when you came on the tv, it'd be all like, i know him—

NARCISSUS. —look, whatever, all right?

ECHO. no, i mean it, for real—

NARCISSUS. —just don't, don't even—cause, girl, what it is, see: you're right. you ain't like me. all you want, when it comes down to it, you just want to get along, you just want to hang back, take it as it comes, don't be wantin shit, don't be askin for shit, don't be gettin up in nobody's face, don't be makin any noise, don't be makin nobody uncomfortable, don't be sayin what it is you got to say—just hang back, fade away, be real quiet, and get by, pray you get by, like that's all you get in this life, like that's all you deserve—well, fuck that, fuck that.

(NARCISSUS' reflection explodes as though a rock had been thrown into a pool, distorts, breaks up. ECHO flees. Darkness.)

THE STORIES OF NARCISSUS
interviews with strangers

(In the darkness. NARCISSUS' reflection is shattering, refracting, pieces of himself breaking up in a dark pool. Voices in the darkness overheard like the rushing of an underground stream, fragments of interviews—overlapping, incomplete.)

M1. fuck that

F2. fuck that

M2. fuck that shit

F2. how it is—tss, fuck it

M5. how it is, right

F3. you want to know how it is

M2. fuck that shit

F4. you want to know how it is

F3. psycho bunched me for everything i own

M1. psycho took all my shit

F2. psycho ripped me off

M2. psycho fucked with my head

F2. psycho called me liar

F3. slut

F4. loser

F2. thief

M5. psycho kicked my ass

F3. psycho sold me bad shit

M2. psycho sold me out

F4. psycho made me sick

M1. psycho took all my shit

F2. psycho laughed in my face

M2. psycho kicked me out

M5. psycho beat me up, broke my jaw

F2. psycho ripped me off

M5. psycho turned me loose

F3. psycho bunched me for everything i own

M2. psycho waited till i was asleep

F4. psycho took all my stuff, everything i own

M5. psycho wasn't even angry, it wasn't even about that

F3. psycho left me in the middle of nowhere

M5. psycho kicked my ass

F2. psycho took all my stuff, everything i own

M2. psycho looked right through me

F5. psycho beat me up, left me for dead in the middle of nowhere, psycho forgot all about me, but i didn't die, right. i didn't die.

(The sound of dead air on tape. The sound of breathing. NARCISSUS is a reflection growing fainter and fainter.)

AND OTHER INCIDENTAL TRANSFORMATIONS

(Late night. ORPHEUS, PERSEPHONE, ECHO and SKINHEADboy are on the periphery of a circle, listening to music on the boombox. They are each in their own world.)

ORPHEUS. i used to know this guy, he got cut up, he bled all over everything, and the next day, you could see where his blood stained the ground, all these flowers sprung up out of nowhere, bright red flowers, right up through the cracks in the cement, flowers like nobody's ever seen before, beautiful flowers, nobody knew their names.

PERSEPHONE. i used to know this girl, she cried so hard, she turned into a river. that's what they said. cried and cried till all that was left was water.

ECHO. i used to know these girls downtown, somebody put a hex on them, turned them into bats. they fly around, you can see them sometimes down in the tunnels, little black bats with sad girl faces.

SKINHEADboy. i used to know this girl, she disappeared. i don't even know where to. i figure maybe she went home or something. and then one night, i see her, out of nowhere, and she's up in the sky, and it's like she ain't even human anymore. it's like she's turned into this star, all bright and sparklin, filled with all this fire and light, and she's so faraway, it's like she's a thousand galaxies away, and i don't even know where she is, if she can hear me.

(PERSEPHONE, ORPHEUS and ECHO fade away. SKINHEADboy is alone in the darkness.)

THE STORY OF SKINHEADBOY
the transformation of iolaus

(Last song on the tape. SKINHEADboy talks into the light. An interview with a stranger. D is watching him.)

SKINHEADboy. yeah, i don't know where girlfriend went to for real. i used to see her around sometimes, but i don't no more. we had this big blowup. I told her, "fuck you, i like dope a hella better than i like you, so deal with it or get lost," and that used to be the truth, too, but it ain't the truth no more. i'm gonna be all clean-living from now on, straight edge and righteous to the bone— you don't believe me? yeah, well, whatever. this lady the other day, she comes up to me, she says, "i want to help you, young man" and i'm like, "that's great, lady, i need all the help i can get," and then she's all like, "do you believe in god?" and i'm like, "hell no." and that was the end of that, jack. she didn't want to help me no more after that—whatever. cause, see, i don't even believe in god anyway. i don't believe in nothing. i mean, what i believe is you can't believe in nothing, and if you do, you're gonna lose for sure, cause shit happens. ain't no big answer to why shit happens, it just does, and you gotta deal with it. or maybe you say, i'm checking out of all this, cause for real sometimes you feel like checking out, ain't nothing to it really—that's how it is some-times, and that's the straight-up truth. *(Lights fades. The*

*afterlight of a flash. The last song ends. Sound at the
end of a tape. SKINHEADboy walks away.)*

D. hey. hey. hold up. hey. where you goin? hey—

(SKINHEADboy disappears. Darkness.)

G AND EURYDICE
—EATING THE FRUIT OF THE UNDERWORLD

*(The sound of breathing. A heartbeat. G is sleeping. EU-
RYDICE is going through his pockets carefully. She
finds matches, paper, an orange—nothing of value to
her. She searches for a watch. No watch. She sees a
charm around his neck, starts to pull. G grabs her hand.
EURYDICE breathes in—the sound of a girl taking a
breath before diving underwater.)*

G. girl, what the fuck are you doing?

EURYDICE *(extricates herself).* i wasn't doin nothin.

G. you think you gonna steal from me?

EURYDICE. baby, don't flatter yourself. you ain't got
   nothin to steal.

G. steal my soul.

EURYDICE. i don't want to steal your soul, old man.

G. steal my heart.

EURYDICE. i don't think so.

G. steal my little good-luck charm. yeah? you like that,
   huh? fourteen-karat gold.

EURYDICE. it's pretty. it's like something a girl wears.

G. baby, i ain't no girl.

EURYDICE. i know that. see, that's what i'm saying. i'm a girl. you could give it to me, and then, i don't know, i'd be like your girl or something.

G. you want to be my girl, huh? what if i don't want you to be my girl?

EURYDICE. hey, man, fuck you.

G. now, why you got to talk like that: "fuck you, fuck you"?

EURYDICE. i talk like i want. and i don't even want to be your girl anyway.

G. well, make up your mind, little girl.

EURYDICE. i don't want to be your girl, old man.

G. tss. you takin it the wrong way.

EURYDICE. i don't even know what you're tryin to say.

G. i'm tryin to say, maybe things ain't always what they seem. i'm sayin maybe you got to look a little harder.

EURYDICE. i'm lookin real hard at you right now.

G. oh yeah? and what do you see?

EURYDICE. you old—

G. —uh huh—

EURYDICE. —but you ain't that old.

G. i ain't that old, i ain't that young. baby, i'm like a god. *(Picks up the orange and begins to peel it.)*

EURYDICE. tss. man, i don't believe you're a god. you're too dirty and snaggletoothed to be a god.

G. uh huh, well, maybe this god ain't that pretty. you think a god's got to be pretty all the time? you think he's got to smell sweet and shit gold? is that what you think?

EURYDICE. i don't know. i don't think about stuff like that.

G. yeah, i know that. that's cause you're young and dumb.

EURYDICE. man, fuck you.

G. "fuck you fuck you"

EURYDICE. man, what do you want from me?

G. for real? girl, i want a good night's sleep.

EURYDICE. that's it?

G. that's it.

EURYDICE. that ain't nothing.

G. now, that says to me, you ain't never had a good night's sleep—

EURYDICE. —tss—

G. —a good night's sleep, that's a treasure. rest your weary bones, free yourself from all earthly cares. but, now, i ask you, how can a man get a good night's sleep when his woman's got one eye open, waiting to rip him off, slit his throat. that ain't no way for a man to live. if a man can't trust, it'll drive him crazy, it'll piss him off, make him meaner than hell. here, you want some orange?

EURYDICE. no.

G. it's good.

EURYDICE. i don't want no fuckin orange.

G. it's good. florida orange, girl, fresh off the tree. here.

EURYDICE. man. you are so weird. i can't figure you out. i can't follow how you think. i can't get inside your head.

G. i like to be able to sleep easy.

EURYDICE. so sleep easy, baby. i ain't gonna stop you.

G. can't sleep easy unless you got some trust. i like to be able to give a person trust.

EURYDICE. tss. can't trust nobody

G. now that ain't true. anybody says that, they don't know. i feel sorry for them. if they can't trust, it's like they ain't even truly lived.

EURYDICE. man, that's bullshit. you got to watch your back all the time. everybody's runnin some scam, for real. everybody wants something. and some folks, it's like they think they can get it for free. they're all like, i love you, shit like that.

G. girl, why you got to talk like that?

EURYDICE. man, shut up

G. cause, see, love ain't shit. it's somethin real and pure and true.

EURYDICE. yeah, that's what they all say. but that ain't even it, see. it's like they want to tell you how it is, tell you how it's gonna be, and they ain't even lookin at you. it's like they're lookin right through you like you was a ghost or something.

G. maybe they see somethin inside you, you don't even know is there yet.

EURYDICE. man, they see what they want to see. it's their own fucked-up trip. ain't got nothing to do with me.

G. girl, you're talkin about love, right, and love is mental. even in the good times, it's gonna make you crazy. and in the bad times, i swear, it's gonna make you wish you could put a bullet through your brain, put yourself out of your own damn misery. and then when it's all gone, you gonna wish you could do it all over again.

EURYDICE. man, for a god, you don't know shit.

G. yeah, yeah, yeah. i'm a fuckin fool for real.

EURYDICE. i'll tell you what i know, for real: don't let nobody get too close, cause i don't care how nice somebody is, fuck nice, you let them get close enough, they'll take everythin you own, your own self even. ain't nobody who won't.

G. some will, some won't.

EURYDICE. tss. ok, you believe what you want, buddha man.

G. i believe that.

EURYDICE. yeah, you believe in love and all that shit.

G. yeah, i do.

EURYDICE. why? you got somebody you love, old man? you got some girl you love?

G. i used to.

EURYDICE. yeah, and what? she broke your heart? she take off, she leave you high and dry?

G. yeah, she broke my heart, but that was a long time ago. she was my lady love, she was my queen, and i loved her with all my heart. so yeah, i believe in love and all that shit. *(EURYDICE tries to pick up the stuff she took from G, and return it to him, but it's scattered all over the place. G approaches her.)*

EURYDICE. here, that's yours. i messed up all your stuff, i'm sorry. *(Time slows down. G gives EURYDICE a piece of orange, and she eats. He gives her another, and she eats. And as she eats, she transforms into something softer, something of who she used to be.)* it's good. where i come from, there's these orange groves, all along the freeway, and the orange trees, they have these little, white flowers, all tiny and lacy-like. man, i ain't even thought about this in so long. i used to go out there all the time, with this guy i used to know, this goofy guy i used to know, and sometimes we'd be out there, and there'd be this wind, and all the flowers, they'd start falling. we'd close our eyes, and laugh so hard. for a little while, nothin else mattered, and everythin was perfect, cause when the wind got up and the flowers started falling, it was like it was snowing, and the air smelled

all of orange, and we thought it was so cool, we thought
it was the coolest thing in the whole world.

*(G caresses EURYDICE like a god caresses a maiden.
ORPHEUS slowly appears like a shadow of the past.
EURYDICE sees him. And the peace and tranquility is
broken. The pulse begins.)*

EURYDICE. look, i got to go, i got to get going. *(Resumes
picking up G's stuff and gives it back to him.)*
G. you always going, huh? that must be a hard thing to
always be going.
EURYDICE. sometimes, it's like if i can just keep moving,
nothing bad'll happen, sometimes, it's like if i stop, i'll
die. *(Starts to go.)*
G. —hey, hold up. what're you afraid of?
EURYDICE. i ain't afraid.
G. what're you so afraid of?
EURYDICE. i ain't afraid of nothing.
G. that ain't true. i know it ain't. cause it ain't about love.
it ain't even about that. you hear what i'm saying? ain't
about nothin 'cept getting out alive. *(Takes out a knife.)*
here.
EURYDICE. i don't want that. i don't want that.
G. girl, ain't nowhere left to run, ain't nowhere left to go.
here, take it, go on—take it.

(EURYDICE takes the knife from G. Darkness.)

ORPHEUS IN THE UNDERWORLD
last song for the queen of the dead

(ORPHEUS and PERSEPHONE are alone. ORPHEUS is in the middle of a story he tells over and over again. Boombox music, low and melancholy.)

ORPHEUS.
> i used to love this girl. she was crazy insane.
>
> i used to love this girl. she was a liar and a thief.
>
> i used to love this girl. she was a wicked little speed-freak.
>
> i used to love this girl. she ripped me off, told me all kinds of lies.
>
> i used to love this girl, we used to fight. i tried to kill her one night.
>
> i used to love this girl, i got her face tattooed on my arm when i was fifteen years old, looked just like her, like a fucking photograph—burned it off myself when i was twenty-one. now i just got a scar, looks like i walked through a raging fire.

PERSEPHONE. —tss. man, you are so drunk.

ORPHEUS. girl, don't say that. it breaks my heart to hear you say shit like that to me

PERSEPHONE. tss

ORPHEUS. girl, why are you always breaking my heart?

PERSEPHONE. man, just shut up. what you're saying, you ain't even makin sense no more.

ORPHEUS. i'm telling you what's in my heart.

PERSEPHONE. baby, if you could hear yourself—you're so fucked up right now, it's almost funny.

ORPHEUS. fuck you.

PERSEPHONE. man, what, what is it? you want me to feel sorry for you? you want me to cry for you?

ORPHEUS. i was going to tell you all about love, remember? i was going to tell you a story about love.

PERSEPHONE. yeah, well, fuck that—i'm sick of your stories, i ain't interested in no more stories about love.

ORPHEUS. oh yeah, you're so hard. you're so tough.

PERSEPHONE. fuck you.

ORPHEUS. girl, why do you talk to me like that?

PERSEPHONE. man, just back off.

ORPHEUS. who do you think you are, who do you think you are talkin to me like that?

PERSEPHONE. oh man, fuck this shit. *(Starts to go.)*

ORPHEUS. girl, where are you going, where the fuck do you think you're going? *(Follows her.)*

PERSEPHONE. man, just back off or i swear i'll cut you up. i'll cut you to pieces.

ORPHEUS. damn. damn, that is so cold.

PERSEPHONE. then call me cold, motherfucker, just don't be getting in my face.

ORPHEUS. girl, oh girl, what am i doing? what are you doing to me, i can't believe what you're doing to me. you look so pretty. it breaks my heart. you got such pretty eyes.

PERSEPHONE. tss. *(As ORPHEUS speaks, he draws closer and closer to PERSEPHONE. A whisper. PERSEPHONE listens as though in a spell. Music begins.)*

ORPHEUS. i could stare into those eyes for the rest of all eternity, i could get lost in those eyes and never come back again—girl, you got eyes that have seen all kinds of shit, all kinds of hurt, you know all about hurt, all

about what it is to have that thing, some pure and precious thing, what that is, to hold it close and lose it anyway, cause it could've been something else, it could've
been different, everything could've been different. i
know you know what i'm talking about, cause i know
you. girl, i know you like i know myself—

*(The music grows louder, becomes distorted. PERSE-
PHONE strikes at ORPHEUS with the broken bottle.
ORPHEUS stops the arc of the blow. ORPHEUS and
PERSEPHONE struggle. ORPHEUS cuts her, and she
bleeds, she falls away like a shadow.)*

ORPHEUS IN THE UNDERWORLD
the shotgun blast of memory

*(The music continues as a pulse underneath. ORPHEUS
is walking toward daylight, blood on his hands. As he
speaks, EURYDICE appears out of the darkness. She
walks behind him like an inverse shadow.)*

ORPHEUS. i used to love this girl. i loved her more than
money, more than pride, more than my own sorry-ass
life—i used to love this girl. and then she ran away. i
followed her to hell and back, and everywhere i was, i
saw a thousand girls she could've been. i held them
close, and looked into their eyes. i said, are you the girl
i'm looking for, are you the one, is she hiding in your
skin? baby, i know that's you.

EURYDICE. don't you turn around.

ORPHEUS. i know the feel of your breath on the back of my neck. i know the feel of your eyes, i know you, i know everything about you.

EURYDICE. you used to know me. you don't know me no more.

ORPHEUS. girl, i have missed you so bad. i have loved you with all my heart. i have never stopped loving you, not for one second. i want to look at you.

EURYDICE. don't you turn around.

ORPHEUS. or what? what are you going to do to me?

EURYDICE. i will turn your heart to stone, i swear i will.

ORPHEUS. i want to see your face.

EURYDICE. man, you wouldn't know me to look at me.

ORPHEUS. don't say that. girl, listen to me. you can come back with me. come back to me and we'll start all over, we'll make it be all right—

EURYDICE. i ain't coming back with you.

ORPHEUS. girl, what are you saying?

EURYDICE. i ain't going nowhere with you.

ORPHEUS. what are you saying to me?

EURYDICE. i forgot you a lifetime ago, you're a bad dream i'm still trying to wake up from, is what i'm saying

ORPHEUS. you're breaking my heart. i have loved you, i have never stopped loving you—

EURYDICE. —don't you turn around—

ORPHEUS. —or what? what are you going to do to me?

EURYDICE. —don't you turn around—

ORPHEUS. —or what, bitch? what are you going to do to me that you ain't already done?

EURYDICE. i will tear you apart.

ORPHEUS. oh yeah?

EURYDICE. i will blow your soul to pieces.

ORPHEUS. yeah. is that right, is that how it's going to be? girl, you won't ever get away from me.

EURYDICE. you think i won't you turn around and see.

(ORPHEUS turns around and sees EURYDICE. The music shifts to an ancient song filled with nostalgia and longing. They dance for a short time. Something of who they used to be, a flickering happiness from a long time ago. Then ORPHEUS looks into EURYDICE's eyes, and she sees who he is and who he has become. The present comes back in a flash. She stabs him with G's knife. Blinding white light. The shotgun blast of memory. ORPHEUS is illuminated, shot through with light. Music ends. Sound at the end of a tape. Darkness.)

THE STORY OF PYGMALION AND GALATEA

(A flash. A moving picture projected into the void, scratched and ancient. No sound except the buzz of a projector. A home movie of a young girl who could have been EURYDICE once, a long time ago. The girl is a small figure, squinting into the sunlight. She waves, smiles out into the future. The camera moves away from her, held by loving and unsteady hands.)

G.   story of a girl i used to know
     story of a girl who turned into an echo
     story of a girl who turned into a shooting star
     story of a girl who crossed the river of forgetting
     story of a girl i used to know
     story of a girl who almost died

story of a girl who came out on the other side
story of a girl i used to know
story of a girl who walked away
story of a girl who got out
story of a girl who walked away, and never looked
   back
and how she changed into something else
and how the old scars, how they grew new, smooth
   skin—

*(EURYDICE is walking away. G watches her go. Dark-
ness.)*

THE TRANSFORMATION OF THE LYDIAN SAILOR

*(A flash. Another moving picture snaps into focus. No
sound except the buzz of a projector. A home movie of
SKINHEADboy playing dead—arms splayed, sunlight
streaming across the lids of his closed eyes. And then his
eyes open, and he smiles. SKINHEADgirl enters the
frame, shoves him and they wrestle on the grass, all
hands and arms and faces, laughing eyes. Soundless
laughter. D is alone in the darkness.)*

D. i used to know this boy. this was a thousand years ago.
   he jumped off a bridge on the other side of town. he
   flew so fast. nobody saw him, nobody heard him. he
   flew so fast, he died before he hit the water. i dream
   about him every night, and in my dream, he's coming
   apart, he's breaking into a thousand pieces, and i go and
   i catch the pieces with my hands, and hold them to the

light and in my hands, the pieces turn into something
else:
    each one tiny and shimmering—
    each one a perfect, living thing—
    and then they slip through my fingers, and swim
      away. i watch until they disappear and all is green
      black water.

*(The moving picture ends. Scratched whiteness at the
end of the film. Then darkness.)*

METAMORPHOSES
an epilogue

*(Voices in the dark call out from all different directions.
Sometimes the voices cut each other off. Sometimes they
overlap. The dark goes back farther than anyone can
see. Light on a wall of polaroid pictures like an anony-
mous shrine somebody left behind. As the voices call out,
the polaroids gradually come clear. From out of the
black-green surface emerge the faces of thousands of
kids. They stare you down.)*

M3. my name is bandit
F1. my name is tina
M2. my name is blondboy
M1. my name is ramon
F2. my name is mohawk girl
F3. my name is lupe
M4. my name is viper
F4. my name is lisa j

M5. my name is crazy todd
M1. my name is ninja b
F5. my name is desiree
M2. my name is david c
F1. my name is rochelle
M3. my name is tiny
M4. my name is paco
M5. my name is skater pete
F2. my name is mai thai
F3. my name is baby punk
M1. my name is tiger
M2. my name is little ray
F4. my name is candy
F5. my name is loca
F1. my name is skinheadgirl
M3. my name is baby j
M4. my name is nazi mike
M5. my name is tweeker shawn
F2. my name is nothing girl
M1. my name is oklahoma boy
F3. my name is jamie b
M2. my name is zero
M3. my name is shadow
M4. my name is scratch
M5. my name is nicky z
M1. my name is dogboy
M2. my name is skinhead steve
F4. my name is happy girl
M3. my name is marco
M4. my name is psycho john
F5. my name is melody
M5. my name is scarface

M1. my name is kaos
F1. my name is disappear
M3. peace
F5. peace
M1. peace
F4. peace
M3. peace

(Silence. A wall of polaroids in brilliant color. Darkness.)

END OF PLAY